County Council

Libraries, books and more.........

Please return/renew this item by the last date due.
Library items may also be renewed by phone on
030 33 33 1234 (24 hours) or via our website

www.cumbria.gov.uk/libraries

Cumbria Libraries

CLIC

Interactive Catalo

Ask for a CLIC pa

D1464959

Published in Great Britain by Avalanche Books, England 2015

Printed by SRP, England

The moral rights of the authors have been asserted.

British Library Cataloguing in Publication Data. A catalogue record for this book is available from the British Library.

ISBN: 978 1 874392 26 2

Supported using public funding by

LOTTERY FUNDED | **ARTS COUNCIL ENGLAND**

Painting is poetry that is seen rather than felt,
and poetry is painting that is felt rather than seen

Leonardo da Vinci

Contents

HOW OFTEN DOES IT HAPPEN
after 'Lunar Eclipse' by Scott Kahn, 2010

that every silver thing is turned to gold
    that reservoirs and railways burn like copper
in the dark of winter's infra-red

that frost is fire, and forests
    are a nerve-machine of birch and blood,
that for a few hours all falls quiet

as wind drops like a child in sudden sleep
    and earth's hair stands on end,
that in the amnesty of moon's blind eye

the world confesses to the stars
    those secrets it would rather hidden
in the deep red ocean of electric dark?

Jane Draycott

THE INSOLUBLE HARMONIES OF COLOUR

The old man sat down against a stump of reflection and began to strip the bark from his torment with a sharp intake of breath.

'I have,' he thought, 'always expected my dour palette to yield a colour bright enough to lead me, with no consideration of the canvas to which I may have applied it. My brushes were the rocks of my ignorance which I did not learn to use with delicacy, and my pigment I hid jealously beneath my contempt for the opinions of others. Now I am alone, and my paint has hardened beyond use.'

As he softly easeled his head on hands tangled like the knuckled roots of an ancient tree, he heard a chorus of sheep bleating a ruminating song while they ambled slowly towards him.

The old man recognised the song at once, and raised his gaze to meet the bearded face of a venerable bellwether.

'It's a simple song,' offered the bellwether as a greeting, with a smile. 'We chew, we sleep, we sing, we amble. The colours of our life are few and muted'

'Yet you paint so beautifully with them,' replied the old man, moved and quieted by the unaffected honesty of the ram. 'I could not match your mastery.'

'We paint what we are able, old man, we make no study of our inability. Our song does not change with expectation.'

'Even so, do you never wish for more than you have?' asked the old man keenly, trying for a moment to comprehend the absence of desire.

'More suns? More grass? More sleep? More song? How would we profit from such a wish, or even the hope that such a wish may be granted?' shrugged the bellwether with a cordial chuckle.

'I have always wished for more,' sighed the old man

apologetically, 'my life has been spent in the pursuit of a formula which would multiply my desires and secure my success. I realise now that my efforts have been wasted. I have not in all my searching found the words to my song.'

The bellwether looked thoughtfully at the old man and attempted to understand the nagging root of his anguish.

'We are sheep,' he began, following a few moments of puzzled headscratching and another good natured shrug, 'we have no comprehension of the meaning of your words.'

'My words are simple. I am a man, and as all men I burned with the desire to succeed. To be better than all other men, to confront my peers with my finery, to arm myself with riches, to cultivate envy among my fellows.'

'To what purpose?' begged the baffled ram.

The old man let loose a long sigh and looked hard into a hazy distance for a reply.

'To be accepted,' he mused at last, 'to be recognised as one of my flock. To follow what was expected of me. To be an example of conformity and to sing a song which everybody knew.'

'You are too clever for me, old man. We sheep are uncomplicated beasts; we greet the sun in the morning, meander over meadows in song, chew the sweet clover and frolic in silvery streams. If we were intelligent animals, maybe we too would cultivate desires and strive for success, but as it is, we can only marvel at the strange magic of your words and carry on singing.'

And as the swelling sun shone like saffron on watery hills, the old man searched the stretched and pine-selvaged skyline for a cooling shower of unformed replies, while the bellwether ambled away with his bleating number toward a fresh green pasture, chewing and frolicking and singing the same song they had always sung.

Chris Tutton

EVERYWHERE YOU SEE HER

Everywhere you see her, who could have been
   Monet's woman with a parasol
who's no woman at all but an excuse for wind –
   passage of light-and-shade we know
wind by – just as his pond was no pond
   but a globe at his feet turning to show
how the liquid, dry, go topsy-turvy, how far
   sky goes down in water. Like iris, agapanthus,
waterplants from margins where, tethered
   by their cloudy roots, clouds grow underwater
and lily-floes, like landing-craft, hover
   waiting for departure, she comes at a slant
to crosswinds, current, against shoals of sunlight
   set adrift, loans you her reflection.
I saw her the other day, I don't know where,
   at a tangent to some evening, to a sadness
she never shares. She wavers, like recognition.
   Something of yours goes through her, something
of hers escapes. To hillbrows, meadows
   where green jumps into her skirt, hatbrim shadows
blind her. To coast, wind at her heels, on diagonals
   as the minute hand on the hour, the hour
on the wheel of sunshades. Everywhere you see her.
   On beaches, bramble paths, terraces of Edwardian
hotels. In antique shops, running her thumb along
   napworn velvet. A nail buffer. An owl brooch
with two black eyes of onyx. Eyes she fingers.
   But usually on a slope. Coming your way.

Mimi Khalvati

I WOULD LIKE TO BE A DOT IN A PAINTING BY MIRÓ

I would like to be a dot in a painting by Miró

Barely distinguishable from other dots,
it's true, but quite uniquely placed.
And from my dark centre

I'd survey the beauty of the linescape
and wonder – would it be worthwhile
to roll myself towards the lemon stripe,

Centrally poised, and push my curves
against its edge, to get myself
a little extra attention?

But it's fine where I am.
I'll never make out what's going on
around me, and that's the joy of it.

The fact that I'm not a perfect circle
makes me more interesting in this world.
People will stare forever –

Even the most unemotional get excited.
So here I am, on the edge of animation,
a dream, a dance, a fantastic construction,

A child's adventure.
And nothing in this tawny sky
Can get too close, or move too far away.

Moniza Alvi

POLYPHEMUS AND GALATA
(After Odilon, Redon)

He looks at her as he loves her,
with the tenderness of the wounded.
As if she were treasure he'd found
in a cave – sapphires, emeralds, amber,
the jewels of her flesh, sleeping.
All looking and no touching,

he's sated with the taste of desire;
but saved from the sadness of having.
His single eye drifts over her
like a moon, its amethyst shadow
bruising the horizon. His one eye.
A single tear. His left hand steadies

the hillside, a door he'll never open.
One kiss would kindle an earthquake.
Stroking her breasts, he'd crush her
like a grape. The love in his look
belongs to a child. One lost in another room.
Locked in his enormous eye. Howling.

Linda France

SUR LA TERRACE
a painting by David Hockney

Limits: distance and near edge,
Here you are contained, and yet
hills and trees delineate
a further world. The curtains
know their place and hesitate,
held back, restrained: open doors
are the best we can hope for.

But listen. Don't turn. There is
another distance within
where the eye shapes, translating
image into imagery:
beyond the curtains, casting
a separate glance and now
a shadow within shadow.

Being and seeing are more
than the best we could hope for:
now all the generous light
is yours. On the terrace you
keep distance and edge in sight
and are them, contained: see how
the shadows bend towards you.

Neil Powell

OPHELIA DROWNING IN THE TATE
after Millais

Once I picked flowers:
bluebell, flax and celandine,
held each one like a tiny hand
spread out in asking.

Through the water meadows:
crowfoot, flag and violet,
I gathered them in a posy,
as if walking to a wedding.

Now, as you look from
your hide outside the wall,
you see me ever drowning;
fitting to the water like my own cast.

You watch me
as I shake the elements,
split the join from air to water,
water back to air.

And, as forever
life shifts round me,
forever is renewed and drained away,
I see your eyes:

blue, green, brown,
the colours of a landscape;
they haunt me from the bank:
bluebell, flax and celandine,
crowfoot, flag and violet.

Simon Williams

UNDER THE VAULT
(The Mason's Bracket, Gloucester Cathedral)

Because we both sit here alone,
she speaks, lips broad unmodish red,
by pinnacles of fretted stone.
'How did they build this, then? 'she says.
'Barrows?' I guess. Pulleys' long jolt —
From blinding glass, spears glare by kings,
Christ's thin bared face crowns ranks of wings.
But where a lesser light is thrown
one ledge, hacked from rough limestone, shows
a boy, who tumbles down the vault.

Apprentice, he hangs from his stone.
His arms are spread, his legs are curled.
Did drink or dizziness descend,
too long a night with his first girl?
High on a platform, weighed by sky,
his master stretches helpless hands
to boy, hair like an angel's streamed.
Unskilled in suffering, alone,
he crouches on unsoftened stone.
His God is dead.   He carves our cry.

Alison Brackenbury

SELF MADE MAN

He picks his palette up, and starts to paint
Invests the canvas with expressive oils
The tight off-white stretched cloth absorbs the daubs
It's recognisable, sharp and severe
His brush fulfils its brief, portrays the traits
The early random-looking lines cohere
By increments an image constellates

My father's mother, as once drawn by him
in brown felt tip when I was in my teens
Beneath today's still life the play of genes
Beneath the leaf - the twig, the branch, the limb

He's traced me back, revealed the family tree
The embedded dna in dynasty

Next session's strokes will see this overlaid
With features I can claim as just my own
The part of me that passes for self-made
Fresh-grown from seeds so very long since sown
In quiet fields which never quite lay fallow
Which never quite wake up, nor ever sleep

Perhaps the me that's me is just skin deep

I hope he doesn't make me look too shallow

Matt Harvey

THERE ARE DIFFERENT WAYS TO ENTER THE GALLERY

Across the neat lawn, through the gift shop,
Where you can buy an apron for your aunt
Or, for fifty quid, a glossy slab of book.
Past the café, where people sip teas and coffees.
Down the light-filled, glass-walled corridor
And up the wheelchair ramp through the sliding doors.
You can stroll with the air of someone revisiting an old friend.
You can rush, clutching your mobile in your pocket,
Breathlessly late for a first date.
You can stand at the door, unsure of what you came here for,
Or you can move in a shoal of words,
Chatting about work, holidays, what she said to him,
Until, suddenly, the paintings come into focus.

Francesca Beard

TEA

inspired by A Ton of Tea by Ai Weiwei

It stands in the centre, a gigantic cube –
countless leaves, a full ton, pressed together.
The block is as high as her breasts,
its corners as sharp as teacups are round.
She holds her face close, tries to inhale
the fragrance of tannin, believes she may have caught
the faintest hint, but then thinks her receptors are most
likely telling her what she hopes to smell. The life
has been squeezed right out of this tea. For all its gloss,
all its solidity, it may well be as dry and flavourless as dirt.
She glances round — checks the security guard is absorbed
in watching a herd of art students – leans in fast, tongue out
as far as it will reach, for one sly, secretive, inquiring lick.

Judy Darley

CURTAINS
for Holly Downing

This is an old light,
where the gleam along a pleat
is geometric, and the shadowed rest
waits somewhere beyond the canvas:
how the painter loved
these fabrics, more than what they dressed

in shining folds; how they glow and steal
life from the flat flesh
and have survived. These surfaces
the painter used to touch,
this linen, silk and velvet,
are her true subject.

They are more themselves than skin;
sloughed, the crumpled cloth
mimics a white smile, a laugh,
lies crumpled on a shelf
or droops from the wooden cliff
to make a painted lap with peaks and troughs.

They are their own stuff
falling, only the draped window
ours, the scenes from ordinary life,
the play, the picture. Even the bed
we all stand round. And these are red
and gold and emerald, and closed on love.

Susan Wicks

ABOUT FACE

Actaeon, you'll pay the price for looking
like a god; athletic, proud, immortal,
Diana, goddess of the hunt, will hound you.
She is too harsh; you should have looked at me.
I am her shadow, black yet fairer than
the mistress, clad in cloth finer than cirrus.
I want you, Actaeon. I wish I were
shroud white; O that you'd notice me and mouth
each monumental curve. Her handsome face
off-guard, you brushed aside the drape to see
how cool she bathed; with the pool's spray, she crushed you
for looking. In this pine-sweet grove, you turned
from man to horned and dappled stag; sentenced.
Look how your fate reflects itself in water.

Look! How your fate reflects itself in water
from man to horned and dappled stag; sentenced
for looking. In this pine-sweet grove, you turned.
How cool she bathed! With the pool's spray she cursed you.
Off-guard, you brushed aside the drape to see
each monumental curve, her handsome face
shroud white. O that you'd notice me and mouth
I want you. Actaeon, I wish I were
the mistress, clad in cloth finer than cirrus.
I am her shadow, black yet fairer than
she is. Too harsh! You should have looked at me.
Diana, goddess of the hunt will hound you
like a god, athletic, proud, immortal,
Actaeon, you'll pay the price for looking.

Patience Agbabi

25

CAVE PAINTING

My skin is wrinkling, growing ochreish;
a whiff of peat rising from the tundra
between my toes. Natural pigments
speckle palmprint, dot scar and mole.

After a bath I trace the shapes
of buffalo, deer, galloping foal;
dry the tribe's prizes
in my cracks – tarsal, oxter, jaw.

That wildness spiralled in my hair
echoes mane, backbone, tail:
not a single strand falling
from the same time's fold.

Certain crannies, my skeleton
is starting to show. In others
it's buried beneath an overhang
of freckle and pucker, lichen-glow.

Sable-brushed, chiselled, smudged,
my body is a palimpsest of stone,
settling back into the earth
she came from thousands of years ago.

Linda France

CÉZANNE TO MONSIEUR VOLLARD

Hold yourself like an apple.
Does an apple stir and move?

I have prepared the chair myself.
You don't risk falling in the least.

One hundred and fifteen hours
but now I must go back to Aix.

On my return be assured
I shall have made some progress.

Portraiture takes time.
To get the hands just right.

As for the mouth and eyes.
When I have them I shall know.

For now the shirt front pleases me.
I'm not dissatisfied with that.

John Mole

WHEN I THINK OF MONET

Monet, my father cherished most, I think,
his bright, audacious palette and subtle élan
completely won him over.
                              Throughout his youth
the only art was the art in his artisan childhood,
bare graft and austerity was by paternal decree,
so when at last he noticed paintings, a flame
stirred.
              He was by then managing a furniture store,
and on many a glazed and heavy afternoon
he'd take to pen and paper, sketching what he saw:
the cluttered showroom, browsing clients, the view
outside his window, where the world moved on;
and from a sober reverence for the Canon,
with its high watermark of all-things-Renaissance,
my father had his own renaissance at Giverny
in the dappled rushy garden with its little humped bridge.

The power of raw paint applied with elegant insouciance
never left him, and marked his own liberation.

Thereafter, he painted for himself with impressionistic slack,
returning again and again to its generous method,
particularly in his final years,
so when I think of Monet or see his work,
I see my father's confidante and friend,
the senior autodidact and true eye,
whose vast and visionary zeal home-tutored
my eager young parent, infusing him

with a painter's grace,
with a peerless taste and judgement.

Lawrence Mathias
.

LILY, HER ROSES IN A BLUE VASE

Lost now, I suspect,
not seen these dozen years.

Enchanting, the rough vivid lines
creased rouches of rose petals.

Remembered blossoms.
Remembered too, there was

uncertainty to the roundness of the bowl
beneath the neck, chill light

of a winter afternoon
falling harsh this side,

the other, certainty
of shadow

seeing the light now
– seeking the light now –

less and less. And Lily's hands
waxy, slipping along

these clumsy crayons, yet leaving
behind them an undiminishable brightness

of lit blue, purple orange, such red
roses, the green of their leaves

pulsing still, still
responding to her breath.

Anne Stewart

ABERDEEN ART GALLERY

*'To help us ensure the comfort and safety of all the visitors to the
gallery please do not let children play with the water in the
fountain. Thank you.'*

Fiona and I were folded into a bed
with a pot hot water bottle under a quilt
that remained damp even at the height of June.

There were *butteries* for breakfast. We scrubbed
the bird bath in a garden of gnarled trees,
and floribunda roses past their best.

Later, we strolled along Rosemount Viaduct
to the gallery to stare at carcasses
by Francis Bacon. I sniggered until reprimanded,

felt the chill of granite pillars against my cheek,
then hop-scotched across a chequered floor
as red paint dripped down the canvases.

At midnight, Gran's stairwell clock began to strike.
Lumps of butchered meat and howls
of conscripts from the war filled the bedroom

as I felt for my sister's spine.
I pressed my feet against hers until the sun rose
and traffic hummed along Anderson Drive.

Anne Caldwell

CAMOMILE TEA

Your cottage always smelled
of wood smoke, turps
and old baked beans.
Washing up was a rare event
and the cabaret was mould.
Your good intentions
grew furzy blooms.
Things in pans developed skins.

You cooked but hardly ate,
lived on the wonky G note
you scratched and bowed
on your battered violin,
sucked fat from the colours
of the same raw-eyed siren
you painted every day.

Back then
I was doped up on camomile tea
and the idea of love,
unable to see the mess
behind your eyes,
thinking I'd saved a man
from drowning.

Gaia Holmes

SUNFLOWERS

Yes, many and beautiful things, Sappho Fragment 24

it's three o'clock on Thursday seventh of August,
a sultry heat that dusts the streets with litter –
an unrelenting dryness in the air –
a flower-seller sits on a step and sunflowers
from Israel fold down into a steel bucket.
A resting place for pollen seeds.
It's then I pause at Van Gogh's sunflowers,
a mural painted on the outside wall.

In the gallery cool rooms display paintings
from centuries unknown to us and I find
a map to find the way to sunflowers,
the ones that dominate and bloom
Outside I buy the sunflowers on offer
rather than a postcard for by morning
when they've dropped and died pollen stains
will remain ground into my hearth.

Wendy French

DURER'S HIPPO

We laughed at Durer's drawing –
too mechanical to be a real creature.
Of course, he'd never seen a hippo,
used his ink to trace the stories
that adventurers brought back
from a continent he couldn't know.
A lesson to us all, we said.

And yet, here it is – a pygmy hippo:
a walking, breathing, excreting copy
of Durer's drawing. So now I ask:
did Durer somehow create this hippo
to authenticate his art, or was it
a memory from some other time
when all the creatures knew each other?

Kaye Lee

BIRD OF THE SEA
after a stone carving by Bridget McCrum

remember
her like
the font
that was leaking
the water
that held
the first flight

she is all of the egg
the shell
the white
the yolk

she is all of the nest
the branch
the tree
the shelter

there on
the ground
she writhes
like a sea
serpent
tarred and feathered

she is all of the pain
of earth
of rock
of sky

she is all of the light
of union
of moon
of metal

Susan Taylor

FORE EDGE PAINTING

James Thomson, *The Seasons,* A wedding gift for EM & DM
London, 1824
*A fore-edge painting is a scene painted on the edges of the pages
of a book. There are two basic forms, paintings on edges that
have been fanned and edges that are closed. A fanned painting
is one that is not visible when the book is closed.*

You know it's there beneath the veil of gilt
and cannot help yourself. Each morning
you take it in your hand, feel the grain
of red morocco, the raised bands pressed
against your palm, let the front board fall
and fan the quire of pages to the left,
spreading the fore-edge with your thumb.

And each time is like the first time –
fields, a bridge crossing water, a road
curving uphill to the walls of a distant town
and the indecipherable colour of sky.

And still it surprises you, how each sliver
of paper plays its part, how even
a closed book can hold a secret.

Lynne Rees

LOOKING AT A KURT JACKSON PICTURE
OF A DELABOLE QUARRY, CORNWALL

Blackness is gathered on the far side
we can scarcely see the light

    the slow trucks dwarfed by black slate
    the sky
    the upper landscape
with its little houses and suggestion of trees
unbelievably far away

standing
so near the glass
(the only thing to remind me
this is someone else's reality)

it's the blue of the water that draws me
to the centre
    light flying out
    light streaming in

When I step back
the side is cut away
to show God's view of the largest hole in England

and the light within the clouds
comes back to me.

Caroline Carver

WOODLAND BURIAL

Thrown water touched him and where it touched it said
his body was the same brownness leaves turn
when autumn is upon us, a swept-up heap
trembling where it stood,
but when the huntress concentrated
trees, tree-shadows, underbrush and bushes made a wood
and it was ever thus, that nothing can be other than as known
by a god, no truth a lie, no death long sleep.

Poised with springy longbow drawn
and back to the sun, the one who had revealed her form
from landscape or eyes
independent as a streak of white paint on a mirror
held him on her gaze
and held the torn canopy of clouds on the water
how she might have kept a spoonful of honey in the warm
fold of her tongue before it dissipated.

Not the greatest possible harm,
which needs to be known and named as such
to achieve its end, not what he fled, but the official crime,
the moment she let her attention crop
those deep recursive avenues of beech to a backdrop
he broke against, confused,
so nothing in the landscape escaped his touch
and nothing left of him was in the picture she composed.

Frances Leviston

DIANA AND ACTAEON

It could be over Strangford Lough
that hoop of sky beyond the archway
with its midsummer blue of a northern country
and corridor of clouds

and Actaeon the servant
standing slack-jawed in the doorway
having stupidly dropped the chocolate tray –
a whole life's wages' worth of china

exploding in confetti
no praying to all the Saints in Heaven
might possibly take back, lift up, undo,
obliterate –

like the sight of his reverend mistress
caught languidly in flagrante
with five of the shyest housemaids
and a cousin from the city.

Stone animals crouched in the dusky gardens
cover their ears. And immediately
he sees, in the uplifted anvil
of her naked heel, his punishment –

whipping, stocking, damaged hands,
a four-day journey south, or, if he's lucky,
a sign slung round his neck
– houseboy for hire –

Sinéad Morrissey

SELF PORTRAIT

Don't deny the first reality in front of you.
David Hockney

It was autumn. All I could do.
Every morning the milky light
lapping at my window. I rose

from the desert of my bed, clicked
on Brahms, Schubert or something else
Germanic; sipped orange juice while

I found the brush, a square I could
fit my face on. For forty-two
days I looked at my lips, my eyes,

their arrangement within the shape
of brow, jaw; sometimes triangle,
sometimes oval. Always hounded,

hungry, abandoned. My poor face.
I discovered it didn't look
how I thought. Old. Blond. Glasses.

And me, still the boy who cycled home
to find his father sitting
in an armchair outside the phone-box.

Still surprised. The white canvas
welcomed me in like a bed.
And I charted my features

like a desert, like pillows, like a dog
waiting to be fed. Every day
for six weeks I painted myself

coming out of the dark tunnel
of myself; that cool oasis,
forty-two faces.

Linda France

PRUNING THE MAGNOLIA

The magnolia is spreading its arms
across the whole garden, juggling pink
goblets, reaching up to the roof.
It was supposed to be decorous,

a Chinese lady by the lake in pink
slippers. But it has loosed itself
from its moorings, taken ship
with a cargo of blooms, broad-leaved

and brash, colonising the delphiniums
and roses, snuffing out the red-hot pokers,
threatening to take over the garden

with a riotous party. So it has to be
pruned, clipped, curtailed,
trimmed like a poodle with a lavish pink bow.

John Daniel

ON THE SAILING BOAT
a painting by Caspar David Friedrich

So on the prow the lovers lean,
She in red velvet, he in green,
Their hands clasped, hot and keen.

Their eyes stare into painted sun,
Who guides the sheltering sail? No one.
Their trip has just begun.

I would rush in, knot the line firm,
To hold them in the glittering storm,
Wrap narrow shoulders warm.

Oh, if you make it, you must land,
Find bills, lost jobs, misunderstand
A child hot in your hand,

And then another. Will you fail?
But look, the sea sleeps, still and pale.
First teach them how to sail.

Alison Brackenbury

BIRD OF PREY
after a stone carving by Bridget McCrum

his back
towards us
is waterfall blazing
a fire of ice

he flew in
here on
permanently folded
wings

heavily
self-possessed
he is too proud
to watch us
take him in
encompass
with round eyes
his blue poise
his otherness

we stroke
his gleaming
plumage
because
he is
so tame

we leave him
where he landed
a lookout
at the window
pent up
against the glass
because he is so wild

Susan Taylor

MAURITSUIS

Snow melting our faces
we left all those Vermeers
behind locked doors –

this time we were too early –
hands frozen together we hid
disappointment in wool gloves.

You rationalised feelings, said
we'd seen most of them before
and then you danced

along cobbled streets pretending
to be drunk to make me laugh.
You mimicked riding a bicycle

into the Holfvijver.
But all I wanted was *The View of the Delft,*
the lady reading this letter.

Wendy French

PORTRAIT IN FADING COLOURS

I painted you
playful in bower shadow
where Whistling Jacks grow
arboured by dusk.

You beckoned me,
reclining clover veiled like
an uncertain bride,

from the time when we were
younger, and watched
lumpsuckers skim the millpond.

Chris Tutton

THE WOODCARVER

An old man is sitting by the Rialto.
He whittles at a figurine,
intricate fingers searching
for the human form
in the gnarl and knot of the seasons.

Each figurine becomes a languid adolescent,
a stretched uncluttered chord
placed once and left to sound
on a grand piano.

He died on a February night,
his stiff body propped on frosty cobbles.
They handled him like antique wood,
manoeuvring him onto a barge.

Then I found one floating. Quizzical,
she unnerves me with her doll's squint.
Washed of river slime, the little idol
is placed on my window sill.

Sometimes on a windless dusk in autumn
when I open the casement,
she sings softly in Latin,
the pale notes moving like candlelight
out over the Laguna Morta to the dead.

Andrew Nightingale

FROM THE LIGHTHOUSE

At the rough-cut edge
of the land, a megaphone
of light, naked
as distress itself,
blares sideways across
the abraded acres of the sea.

If this were a book, you'd call it
one with a preface and afterword
and a bright ribbon
to mark your progress
from the underworld of the past
to the thin air of the future.

Lawrence Sail

ENGINE OF HISTORY
after 'Le Grand Cheval' by Raymond Duchanp-Villon,
a Bronze dating from 1914

A sound-poem set to the soundtrack of a horse's hooves,
which slowly morph into the pulse of a tank's engine.

Silence. And from it, twist
Shoulder, flank.

    Heart-beat and steady
Hoof-plod; and the coulter

    Parts the clay, its fragrance
Winding downriver.

    Hot horse lather.
Quarters, croup, hock

    Thrust up; the straight
Cannon plunge; a piston

    Pounding, its contradiction
The bend, break, flex

    Of water's curve and cusp,
That beautiful, blind striving.

    Beat, heart, and arch
Crest; shoulder

    Bow till the living spine
Uncoils; its engine –

Cog, chain-link, track-plate –
Parting the clay, the river

Dragging its stink –
Sweat, dung, machine-oil, corpses –

Onwards – relentless,
Unswerving – into silence.

Katrina Porteous

MONUMENT

Imperial London. The bronze horses rear
in autumn's sunlight on the highest ledge,
the driver wreathed. Peace? Triumph? But I see
the hoof-tips slip, unsteady, past the edge.

Alison Brackenbury

PAINTED BIRD, FOUND IN A ROMAN GRAVE

'They left this cockerel by the head
so Mercury could reach the dead.
The cockerel is his messenger.'
I thought, after the expert spoke,
they set is so, as in a bed,
the child would see it, when he woke.

Alison Brackenbury

HEAD OF NEFERTITI

Dropped from my ear to the ground
It exists on the concrete, on the pavement

of the wet day – the day which began
at 5a.m. with dawn breaking across

the light switch in the bedroom –
the sky red, my father after ninety

years of mornings would have said was a warning.
And now rain tips down to bury it further

into the kerb but for all we know
it's comfortable there – gold to concrete.

It's found a place away from where it began,
gold mines of Africa, caste into this head,

packed and flown across heavens to land on my carpet.
I have been careless; a card from you lies in my drawer.

Maybe the ear-ring runs with the river along the old roads.
This is the river that seeps into our cellar on dark days

when lightning storms overhead.
These are the days that will challenge the way we used

to talk at night about love and coincidence and names,
the graveyard that backs onto our kitchen garden.

Wendy French

ANNIVERSARY
after Paula Rego

When I am sleeping things occur. You come
Back from the dead, I lift the big stone off you
With my dream fingers, it weighs no more than a feather.
You stand and stretch and look, though not at me
Because I am asleep. You walk right through me.
You leave prints in the dirt and your shadow
Moves beside you, shadow cast by moonlight,
As though an intimate has come back with you
Holding your hand, sharing your pulse and posture.
You have upon you the smell of mildew and soil
And that sweetness you always wore is palpable and yes,
You walk right through me and I feel your heart again
Pommelling the bone bars inside your chest
And in your throat and lungs the rasping that killed you
Not the phlegmy prelude to your funeral,
More now like a hoarse hymn of resurrection.
Down at the cemetery gate you linger,
Step out into the road with its yellow lamps,
Look, your shadow also, towards town, then up hill.
No one familiar. No one, not even a car.
You turn and come back in, and go back home
To the place we put you, marked, and in time forgot,
Walking right through me you find the spot
Among the pine shrubs, by the wind-shaped oak,
Lie down again and pull the soil tight up
Under your chin, and close your hazel eyes.
The big stone weighs too much for me, your shadow
Helps me replace it and daylight comes in.

Michael Schmidt

DAWN, NOON AND EVENING
after Caspar David Friedrich

Dawn

The watery light in the saturated air
Is sun dissolving as it rises. Might be an hour
Before you see the fire and even then

Flat, white, cold, a thin coin
In appearance like the water-commanding moon.
Shores and forests and bare mountains

Are biding their time of appearance but he, the drylander
Who cloaks his bones in a soft moist skin
Is rocking already on the shallows of an inland sea.

Water is best, and he is mostly water. But now
He must concentrate the light of his mind and his clever hands
On landing fish. I imagine him not even muttering

Encouragements to himself though the soul in him
Fervently wishes he would halloo
Far and high and wide and again and again.

She would love to know whether anywhere around
There is another being at all like her
Inquisitive, sociable, uplifted, always wanting to see

And whether shoving off at dawn into the fog
In a trunk with a pole and a little sail of breath
He is heading towards some society or away.

Noon

As I painted this scene I saw beyond any doubt
We shall never be at home here whatever we do.
Noon was dull, a mild grey, it will not smite you;
And sylvan hasn't meant savage in our land for years;

All's softened; but as I did my copse of trees
They dwindled my two little humans almost to nothing
And the path I made, such a pleasing curve,
steadily bore her away, far left. I saw

This continuing without me, the trees taller,
Sky damping the earth with fears even at noon,
Absence, all my doing. Little man far right
Cross the dumb field while you can, wish her good day.

Evening

Dawn was dull and noon and the brief afternoon
Dull and the pale light general. Only now
Does the source descend into their vision
And with this moderate effulgence quits them

For ambling along companionably
All day in a dark wood. The last trees stand tall
Like bars but they'll squeeze through and arm in arm
Tumble in glory into the common fosse.

So much for the sheep. Take it from me, Chloë
Goats have more fun. Earth is not lagged all around
With fog, she will unbutton you slowly or
Rip, if you can't wait, the long dress of pale cloud

On pastures of naked sky and as for woods,
The light beech, the dark holm, how your slopes will love
The many textures of bedding. Couple, sleep
And crawl in the morning to the grassy hem

And there, cross my heart, I will show you a light
Giggling with the breezes, flirting with midges
And freshly out of websilk, dew and frogspit
Shape you up desire again, hard as a hole.

David Constantine

STANHOPE A. FORBES AT NEWLYN
after 'A Fish Sale on a Cornish Beach', Stanhope A Forbes

Mirror, mirror,
he said, when he saw the beach
and looked across it.

He wanted to reach
hold of sky, by painting
sea ghosting the sand.

Its gilded plane
was a perfect foil
for his ambition.

He set up the easel,
pegged it down against wind,
in defiant mood.

He would lift that shine
and place it on his canvas
in a gesture of light.

Women were caught
in his thrall, as hands landed
spectacular fish.

Delicate pastels
for skins of catch and girl; both
salt water creatures.

Men coming home
reeking of fights with nets.
Men not coming home.

Susan Taylor

MORE WATER THAN LAND

after an untitled abstract painting by Katy Webster

She half-closes her eyes so
the world blurs against the window,
hills and fields transforming
to a view that seems more water than land.

The scene is so familiar she almost inhales
the sweet, damp smell of crops
soaking up the deluge; puddles mirroring
the fading sheen of an evening sky

Daylight has already begun to ebb,
inviting night to creep in, and her own
reflection to supersede the countryside
of memories she journeys through.

She knows that not long after her face
becomes an apparition haunting the glass,
she'll arrive back in the place she grew up;
something tightens in her gut at the thought.

She closes her eyes fully,
blocks out the rain-smudged scenery,
feeling only the *thud-ah-thud, thud-ah-thud*
of the train rushing her home.

Judy Darley

AN INCONSEQUENTIAL PHOTOGRAPH

The way the camera's angled makes it hard to see
whether the gin's half full but the tonic's empty
beside the blackened saucepan which holds gnocchi
next to the sausage fry-up.

It's hard to see whether there are cherries left on the trees; perhaps
we've eaten them as they dropped, dark, almost black, into our
                                                            hands –
you're never in the photographs, claiming you're the only one
who can hold the camera steady.

It's hard to see who's talking but there's laughter as we remembered
the slowworm that slithered through the stillness when we arrived
and you threw the blue cloth over the table to make life respectable
before adding forks, neatly polished glasses.

We're poised like a summer sketch found in an old notebook
and I think blue cloth, cherries, against a back-drop of horses
who canter to the fence in the hope of apples or recognition
of their part in this frame.

It's hard to know how the photograph popped up on to my screen
without being called; it's distracted the task in hand and now hours
have been wasted looking for the sign of a cherry, horses, common
                                                                nouns
that were important, that stay fixed.

Wendy French

TILLY AND CLIFF
after 'Tilly and Cliff' by Lal Hitchcock

You're made out of odds and I'm made out of ends
We're cast-off bits and bobs but we're more than just friends
We have so much in common, we both know how very odd it is
To be composed of off-cuts & extraneous commodities

Your various parts all add up to a wonderful sum
They're all fit for purpose, just not their original one
You're more than the sum of your parts. You know what a man want,
You stepped out of the sea like a Bond-girl. But not all at once.
        You're the woman I want. *You're the man I adore*
        I'm so glad you washed up on my shore

You're quite simply one of my favourite people
An incremental immigrant – not an illegal
We can still share a thermos, and magical moments
If you don't mind the age-gap between my components
        It there's a doubt in your mind then let me reassure:
        I'm so glad you washed up on my shore

I like your beach-comb-backed hair and your broom brush bristles
When I kiss you it's like being tickled with thistles
I like your fishnet fullness and your frontal bumps' protuberance
Although they're made of plastic they're a natural exuberance
        When you come in to view I can't help but go 'phwoar!'
        I'm so glad you washed up on my shore

You're my Mr Right – you're my Ms Even Righter
My High Tide high five you're my love-at-first-sighter
You're more, I adore you, you're my Mr Rightest
You're made out of debris and I'm made out of detritus
      Our parts may wear out but our love will endure
      I'm so glad you washed up on my shore

      Let's not be afraid of the facts, turn and face them
      If bits should drop off we can always replace them
      If the blues come along we'll just turn and chase them
      Away...

Though tenderly assembled we are neither of us cosseted
We've been buffeted and bashed about and bashed about and buffeted
I'm sorry for your troubles but I'm glad you were deposited
Along the same high tide line and your attitude is positive

You're winningly winsome. *You're handsome and then some.*
Are there finer men out here? Cos I've never met them
You can keep your fine fellows from Topsham and Epsom
I prefer my men from flotsam and jetsam
      You've the coastal charisma that I can't ignore
      I'll say it again as I've said it before
      At the risk of appearing a terrible bore
      I'm so glad you washed up on my shore

Matt Harvey

SUSAN MARTIN, PAINTER'S WIFE

Forty-five years we were married,
years as stormy as those extravagant paintings
he seemed to adore more than me.

I remember long hours reading aloud,
as he messed with his palettes and brushes,
the lurid fumes of oils fisting my lungs.

The focus of his eyes set his visions on fire,
as sunlight through glass. He'd fan the crimson
flames. I'd melt; continue reading.

Soon I was too busy for *Paradise Lost:*
six children to rear, three to bury;
and money stretched as tight as canvas.

A pity his purse never matched his popularity.
I shiver at the expense of his plans for London
that came to nothing. So practical, black and white.

Now he's dead, there's little left. All our gifts
from kings and lords and princes sold at auction.
Just some chaotic pictures, a fading name.

And me, a rheumatic old woman,
telling the tale of someone else's life,
waiting for a death to call her own.

Linda France

CLAPPER BOARDS
after Cape Cod Morning by Edward Hopper

It took twenty years or more
before the trees gave up their souls
and bodies to the woodcutter.

Summer, autumn, winter and spring
seasoned the sappy wood before
they cut it into boards

to build the house and paint it white,
catching the light which seemed to fall
sideways on her waiting face

as she stood for hours in the place
where she could watch
the ever-empty sea.

Alwyn Marriage

STITCHING TWILIGHT
im PDG
after Paul Klee Twilight Flowers

This could be a new embroidery,
one you made from a grandson's drawing –

see the bird, its beak open
to drink in the last of the daylight

while a scarlet tulip, believer in spring,
leaps over a bonsai wattle tree

stooped beside your fat–as–a–donut cat
who plays ball with the end–of–day sun,

and the giraffe is surely the one from Dubbo Zoo
where we ate cold pasties: it was after Heidi's wedding,

remember, a pause on our three day journey home
when every hill was purple from Paterson's curse.

But it's only a postcard that lies
on the cold tiles by our London door

and though the reds and greens, orange and blue
zing with the heat of your Wimmera home

and the bird seems to be a kookaburra
passing on his favourite joke

when I turn the card over it's an owl
that spells out your name –

you couldn't have sent this card.

Kaye Lee

SELF-PORTRAIT WITH CROPPED HAIR
after Frida Kahlo

There was a grinding of black blades
in that sixth room of hell
I fell into after you left.
I sharpened the scissors until
my bedroom became the House of Knives.

Then I sat on the crazy-yellow chair
and watched my snake-locks rise
from the floor, dance like musical staves
and sing that old folksong you used to whistle –

Look, if I love you, it is for your hair,
now you are bald I love you no more.

Pascale Petit

SELF PORTRAIT
from a German Expressionist woodcut

Picture your face in reverse,
unnoticed, undone and hack away,
leave aside the knife for wrist slitting
but take a blade that understands
the casual interplay of black and white,
or 'light and dark', if you must add tone
to the extremes of howling sorrow,
blank pain. You have to bear in mind,
what to keep, what to lose, it is you
after all, escaping from the wood block,
cushioned in soft paper, squeezed
then screwed down into this life.

Bruce Barnes

MEAN SQUARES
after Mark Rothko, Seagram Murals

Mean squares, oblongs of spite,
Staring down with steak-knife eyes.
I'd have rather had the salad, but it didn't cost much less
And this is our anniversary.

Malevolent mouths, stop your throbbing.
No one looks, all they see are burgundy schemes.
Only some tourist, with her blinking spouse,
Hears your furious trombones.

I could rescue you,
But you are closed and will not open,
Marooned in this room, where Mozart plays in time
To tines on teeth and glass on damask.

I did not come here for the crab cakes, the celebrities.
Twenty years ago, I met a young man
In front of a doorway, cousin of yours,
Same wine-dark wound, same charred raft.

He, that slight stranger, blinked and said
'It's not what I thought.'
Closer we came, further in, understood,
With capillaries, lumen, gut, everything is love.

We walked through Central Park, past the summer theatre,
Somewhere, a man, in German, singing about rescue.
His voice soared all around us, into sky.
If you look, you can catch it in my eyes.

Francesca Beard

ICE AGE ART - AN EXHIBITION

First, as I peer, I hear the scrape
where the sharp stone's edge cut to bone
beneath the hair, the skin, the fat.
Next, deer or bison come

with fragile legs and capes of fur
scratched, like the shadow's dancing line,
tossed heads, recalled by stiffening hands,
while the last oil burned down.

Why did the spotted horses run?
Who were the men with wolves for heads?
Quick dream, before half-frozen beds?

I do not think they shaped stone gods,
or carved for hours to ward off harm.
The East wind blows down Oxford Street.
They made these things to keep them warm.

Alison Brackenbury

LAST NIGHT I DREAMT

inspired by work by Paul Smith

Tonight I dream
of docile lions that
feed from my hands
lie hotly on my feet,
let me run my fingers
against hot, flicking ears,
and gaze at me with looks that say
'I could swallow you up tomorrow'.

Tonight I dream
of soaring through a sky of stars,
through frosted clouds
and under bridges,
over city spires that
catch at my trailing toes
and warn me that at any moment
I might forget how to fly, and fall.

Tonight I dream
of sleeping in the treetops,
cradled high above the land
by branches that rock
me gently with the wind,
each creak whispering
a reminder my fears could cause
this bed to break and cast me down.

Tonight I wake
to find you standing in shadow,
a stalagmite beside our bed, still-sleeping
eyes be-fogged, bewildered.
When I call your name, you roar
incomprehension. I touch my palm to your chest,
and you allow me to entreat you back into
the safety of our marital bed.

Judy Darley

IN RESPONSE TO THE SEA
after 'The Sea' by Emil Nolde

The night you picked
was purple-graped
Hanging, ripe,
around our shoulders
The beach was a grave
of fruit stones and bones
and we washed our feet
in salt water
slapping them
like drowning fish
in the shallows
We talked sweetness
until the wind took it
sucked what was left
of the fading orange sun
Pushed the waves away
with our eager tongues
Swallowed the dusk
left our clothes
and let the sea take us.

Sarah Miller

AFTER KANDINSKY

Yellow, Red, Blue – (1925)

'When you arrive at a state of shock,
the paradox of colour will balance you'

Watch the animal eyes that whisk corners
faster than an angel breathing passwords
in a mesh of yellow. Cloud-sure, life flags itself on.
Circle after circle is mapped in the mystery
of a line quicker than an arrow, shot from left to right,
the dark corners turned in on themselves,
while the sea advances up the cliffs.

Presently a cat walks tall out of the waves,
eyes open, heading for the fire at the centre,
the red waves fanned, turned crimson,
surrounded by purples that ferry
the jigsaw's spell. Choices multiply,
resonate, form patterns for love-songs
the heart claims again and again.

In the background, dark moons, resilient,
juggles patchwork squares, lines, and curves.
Light bounces off them as finally the perfect blue
you've been waiting for, dips, tumbles
into the still of the storm, among reds, purples,
all shades – this country you keep coming back to,
that walks you home to yourself.

Katherine Gallagher

MEMORIES OF FLIGHT
(PICTURES AT AN EXHIBITION)

1 The Rose Lagoon

Vespers, and a black moon.
But look – here's a softer piece:
for a friend in a faraway country

a rose lagoon, and from its core
a light mist rising, warm and teasing,
a genie in a gilded bottle.

Tell me how swallows navigate home,
over and over – those few grammes
against all the implacable ocean.

11 Evening Light

This painter makes swallows. In a mirror
a nightingale practises migration

and in his turquoise lagoon
flamingos shimmer with pigment.

He is Icarus. At the point of his brush
everything's possible. In the tip of him.

Later she'll oil his shoulders,
slide her hands lower, release him.

For a moment he'll believe in flying.

Day turns to night, and in the blink
of an eye he knows that

the atoms that bind them together
also hold them apart.

Roselle Angwin

ASPHODEL

With the liniment of this
brush I could raise you to

the carnival of your colour;
steal you from nothingness,

reach inside your garden and
throw petals of daylight onto

your sleep; dream your little
scalloped eyelids open with a kiss.

Chris Tutton

TWO NUDES

I want it to always be like this,
neither night nor day, just the two of us

in the one bright place in the desert.
We left our clothes in the city; just brought

this red blanket to lie on, fold ourselves in
if the air turns crisp. Your hand smoothes my hair

till I am calm again. Vines and roots
tangle and twist like all the little miracles

busy beneath our skin. I can feel the push
of your toes, the balm of your foot on my thigh,

your flesh warm as a fresh-baked loaf.
This is where I feel most at home, my head

in your lap, my country all about me:
the heart of things; a world at war.

       Frida Kahlo 1939

Linda France

O GOD WHO MADE

Almighty God who made the land
and sea but did not make these canals,
look down from your attic at this latticework

of water, how in the dank and damp
a barges' bow-lamp frisks the embankment.
See how the star-spoked web expands –

a sash round the city's waist, there where the hand
rests close to the heart like Rembrandt's Isaac
and his young Rebecca, palm spanning out

beneath her own, his sleeve a match-flame,
living sun, a stellar flash,
of a honeycomb alive on the canvas.

The fingers of the water fan out
in their channels, search the darkening map.
Where is she now, the girl? Hold the candle

closer to this patch of night, its amber
heart a star, its yellow patterning
visible from space and every watching planet.

Jane Draycott

PRAISE TO THE PHOTOGRAPHER
for Jason

Eyes shuttered, face first,
Move without permission,
Towards thresholds.
Disrupt stories by listening.
Lose your self.
Suck it up.
Focus on sharp objects,
On your last nerve, react
To the ruined, insouciant world.
Skin your trust against relentless futures.
Let everything you touch freeze and blur.
Sacrifice the moment, each moment.
Assassin, thief, betrayer,
Blink with your human scales
Into the upstream, thrashing current of days.

Francesca Beard

OUTSIDER ART

A woman with a blindfolded nose
holds a woman with a slit for a mouth.

*

A man segmented like an anatomical chart,
a pavement, the shell of a tortoise.

*

Unpublished books of hair, string, leaves,
seasoned and cooked in the oven.

*

An Eiffel Tower of rough timber and nails,
Upside-down cows.

*

Her face looks one way, her eyes another.
Her cheeks rucked like a landscape.

*

Lightly shaded,
a simple door, two panels, a key in the lock.

*

A surface covered and covered and covered,
scrolled and scribbled all over.

*

Brooding gargoyles in torn scraps of fabric,
dyed arms outstretched.

*

Hundreds kneeling without any knees.
Heads, just heads. Sparrows and snowfall.

Moniza Alvi

THE IMAGINARY MUNICIPAL GALLERY REVISITED

A research assistant on Malraux's Musée Imaginaire,
Jorn first conceived of his own imaginary museum,
the embryonic Institute for Comparative Vandalism;

his imaginary book *10,000 Years of Nordic Folk-Art*
noting folk topology's snaky roads, spirals, mazes,
revolutionary cycles, identical exits and entrances;

his imaginary exhibition called *Die Welt Als Labyrinth,*
a three-day derivé co-ordinated with walkie-talkies,
would escape its gallery to rebuild the city in words –

'The Labyrinth that is the Production of Situations'
built by Oulipian rats for the purpose of escape,
to be food for real snakes in this imaginary garden.

Ian Duhig

TRIANGLES

*in response to Buckminster Fuller exhibits at Barbican Art
Gallery*

Angles, stacked rows, restless, honeycombed,
Triangulating, replicating, repeating, reinventing
Patterns.
Heptahedrons folding out to synapses, jazz, foam on sand,
Grains, clouds, pebbles, bubbles and spangles,
Of waves of sound, of light.
Cells in the leaf, coral reefs, whorls of skin.
The world you are in
Is elegant, eventually equilateral, laughing.

Francesca Beard

BEACHCOMBER

There was never any danger
in her life
but everything she picked
and pocketed from the tide line
was broken and dreamed of biting:
Whimbrels' bills, the jagged necks
of Jim Beam bottles,
gulls' eggs, fluted clavicles
and slack crabs claws.

The horizons
of her landscapes
were full of holes.
Buds shrivelled and flaked
before they had time
to bloom.
Wonky suns slipped
down the skies,
cracked and seeped
their broken golds
across her crayoned fields.

She was one of those girls
who Sellotaped crushed moths
into her school-books,
one of those girls
who let fruit rot in her satchel

before it ripened,
one of those girls
who scrawled her anxiety
into wet cement
and left it to set.

Gaia Holmes

DEPTH OF FIELD

after David Noonan's 'Untitled' tapestry,
woven by Tapestry Foundation of Australia

I believe she is weaving a white peacock's tail
out of a tumbling waterfall of silk
semi-transparent

A bunch of spring blossom presents itself
as if in my hand. Huge thorns are in danger
of tearing my wrist

yet there are no thorns, just slim leaves
wilting, caught at an angle
on thick stems, pale with sap

This upright woman and the lower one could be sisters
and the third woman could be a man
a celebrant or some other being

set loose from imagining, a face
buried deep in a hood
somewhere lost

and bearing what could be metal
edible, or tender
something powerful

sacramental or soothing,
something scarred, crushed
organic

a thing for weaving
or woven into the lizard skins
of the forest

Susan Taylor

PORTRAIT OF THE MASTER WITH MISSING TABLE

You can see where it's been painted out,
a gap in the midground of the rich interior –
too much tiled floor. The Master
stands erect by a high-backed chair
with leather seat and arms, behind him
a gothic window, anonymous bare trees,
glimpses of a river hazed with gold.

He wants to sit and read but he
must always wait beside the missing table
where he might place the cumbrous book
he carries in his arms. The eyes betray
serious displeasure – he frowns,
as if to ask *Who took away my reading table,*
leaving me to stand and hold this book?

Clare Best

CHRIST IN THE HOUSE OF HIS PARENTS
after the painting by John Everett Millais

His cousin John was summoned from next door
to bathe the wounded hand and staunch the blood,
careful not to spill his precious water on the floor.

It was probably a nail or rough splinter of wood
that pierced the child's skin and made him cry in pain,
so that his mother rushed to where he stood

and knelt beside him, insisting yet again
that a carpenter's workshop is no place for boys
She reasoned with him, trying to explain

that hammers and sharp nails should not be used as toys,
and if he had any sense at all he'd take a little more
care of himself. But all the arguments she employs

fall on deaf ears, he's thinking only of the sick and poor
and the lost sheep waiting for him just beyond the door.

Alwyn Marriage

LIFE DRAWING WITH CARYS

I am two dark notches
in a head like a small pumpkin.
Then she gets stuck.
What about my neck?
She looks at me and draws a shelf
under my pumpkin chin, arms and legs
unravelling from it like loose wool.
How to make sense of all this?

I wobble on the threads of my legs
until my arms with their little knots of fists
start to push against the edges
of the paper and out into the room.
It seems I can be
anything, even the moon
staring through the tall window
like the eye of a fish.

Lynne Rees

THE ART OF THE HANDKERCHIEF

Whenever Sebastian Locke blows his nose,
he is reminded of Professor Mouchoir's

lectures on the pier. How the eminent gent
discussed dribbles and stains; gale force

sneezes; the insouciant manner with which
the Amazing Baldini whipped a red silk

handkerchief off his gold–ringed fingers
to reveal a dove startled by the footlights.

How he contrasted the sublime and cor blimey:
the cream pocket square drooping like a lily

with the knotted hanky as seen on the sands.
How he ended his talk with the drying of eyes:

the volume of water that could easily fill
the Great Lakes of the Northern Americas.

The salt pyramids stretching across time.
Sadness. The incalculable sadness of it all.

Michael Bayley

THIS GALLERY

Raindrops fall
against the windows, cast
anxious shadows over the Masterpieces:
you tell me off
for allowing my umbrella to drip
across your perfect parquet flooring.

I want to run my fingernail against
the soft wax of Anish Kapoor's imaginings,
trace my tongue across his grooved
landscapes, press thumbprints into his
abstract-thoughts-made-physical,
or peel the wax right off;
reveal the soft edible layers beneath.

Your horror amuses me; my laughter disquiets,
then, unexpectedly, entices you.

We reach an understanding as I stare into
one of Turner's stormier seascapes. You come
up behind me, tuck two icy fingers into
the soft warmth at the inside of my elbow,
and for a moment I'm underwater,
fighting to break the surface. Draw breath.

Judy Darley

GESSO

Scrape him off your life,
the wrong colour on your canvas.

See how he has seeped into
all your bright birds
and made them grey.

See how he has soured
all your summer skies
and bleached the sun.

Forgive him.
He has turned
all your ripe, red apples
in to stone.

Gaia Holmes

TITANIA WINGS
after Titania, *John Simmons*

These wings are my passport to nakedness.
They are not angel's but fairy's wings.
The paintbrushes and pigments he uses on them
persuade me that joy can be squeezed
in drops out of my skin into your eyes
so you love me as long as my young body
lasts in his frame – long as anyone knows.

The blue fall of water-silk over my arm covers my legs
and Venus's mound in a shimmering smoke-shift.
In the moony studio light – I am really like that
but the woodbine and violets are normal-sized flowers
scaled up into giants to make me look small.
My hair is a steady spray of gold and the veil and my tresses
suggest moon and sun curling gently upon one another.

I know my nipples surpass the perfection of any bud.
I plant my feet firmly down on the leaf's fringe
but they run down the beach of his looking
and flutter-kick through the wondering tide in his eyes
behind to wherever your thoughts find a place
with Titania unclothed –
her wings in your face.

Susan Taylor

TULIPOMANIA

after Rory McEwen's watercolours on vellum

What binds you is a puzzle,
nub ruched in chlorophyll;
vellum high-drama – those push-me
pull-you strokes I must pluck out
my eyes to elucidate.

> *Old English Striped Tulip 'Sam Barlow'*

Flamingoed half to death,
queer, alcoholic pink,
I accuse you a keeper of secrets,
kisser of bruised lips,
inarticulate with thirst.

> *'Columbine' Bybloemen Breeder*

Darling, your encrypted coral
is wave and particle, wet
and dry. You are a creature
of the sea, plus its shell-like:
that old venetian paradox.

> *'Julia Farnese' Rose Feathered*

You break with tradition,
expose what you wouldn't
even mention as flaws, delineate
your own *vade mecum,* risk
the interior, canyon and gorge.

'Mabel' Flamed

Cheeky, sticking out your bum,
knowing I'll chase you forever,
never catch up – licked
sherbet's tingle and fizz; chameleon
of blown, exploded glass.

Tulip 'Red and Yellow'

Your life as a parrot
is a sly disguise, utter nakedness;
raucous, a knack for tricks,
showing off, sudden flight.
Without you, I'm bereft.

'James Wild' Feathered

Neither vegetable nor fruit,
are you the devourer
or the devoured? No one
could be more open
without stumbling into dying.

'Helen Josephine' Rose Breeder

Given in to gravity, you
let yourself go – your widowed
grains of pollen, full stops
on thin air. I count six tongues,
nothing else to be mad about.

'Dying Tulip 1 '

Linda France

UNBORN

He squats like a sulky toddler,
his too-big head plotting for ways
to sever the cords that hold him
in a place that is waterlogged
and dark.
                    See how he curls as if
in angry defiance. He doesn't guess
the fight toward freedom: the pushing,
squeezing, the stranglehold of cold
dry air, blasts of light, nor that he'll
lose the metronomic beat of seconds
soothing the hours. And though he
might have planned his breakout
it's plain he's not ready, his position
is all wrong.
                   It's too late. We can't
leave him to grow, he'll never learn
to live: his only existence will be
in Leonardo's *study of the foetus
in the womb.*

Kaye Lee

OWL AGAINST WALLPAPER,
PERCHED ON THE ARM OF A NUDE

There is no prey here;
no mice, shrews or voles,
nothing my radar face detects
that I could drop on in the night.

The trees don't give protection;
no shade, no background of leaves,
nothing as backdrop to the sounds
my snow-silence absorbs.

This branch has flesh for bark;
I needn't grip it tight to feel the heat.
When I turn my head I see
fresh curves among the leaves.

This forest becomes her
as I become the dark each evening.
It's not all camouflage;
it's the way we stand and wait.

Simon Williams

AFTER KATHE KOLLWITZ

It's the mothers that suffer,
inherently, as if it were
a gruesome privilege to be
living with their children's years,
of peek-a-boo and hide and seek,
that are still-born, irretrievable.

It's the men who will suffer,
consistently, as if it were
their poisonous birth right to see,
ideals, twisted and rearranged,
go heads bowed in self-disgust;
worse still, they know they can change.

It's art that can suffer,
perpetually, as if the world spoke
with an acid enough tongue
to lick & gouge out copper plate.
But the soul's sticky varnish
can draw out figures from their dark.

Bruce Barnes

THE GESTURE

To step forward to the canvas then back from it
without making a mark, and to do this
again and again as the paint on the brush
thickens, as my eye, my hand, my heart
refuse to repeat the gesture once made freely
with a synthesis of joy. What Auerbach called
the safety net of manner could be mine
if I admitted it, to break my fall and rest there
saved by repetition. What you might say
is 'Nobody paints like him, amazingly prolific
for his age, such energy, such vision', easy words
like that, but exactly so, I should indeed
be nobody with nothing left to show but a blank
and vacuous deception. No, I'm not ready yet.

John Mole

THE STONES ON THORPENESS BEACH
Guy Gladwell: 'Thorpeness Dawn'

O luminosity of chance!
Light spins among the spider-plants
As sand or amber glow seeps through
Tall windows of a studio,
While on the beach in random rows
The enigmatic stones compose
A silent staveless variation,
The music of regeneration.

Relearn astonishment, and see
Where splinters of eternity
Still glitter at the water's edge,
Beyond the tideline's daily dredge
Of flotsam: plants and creatures who'd
Survive this stale decaying world,
And stones worn smooth as solid tears,
Each crafted by a million years.

Or dusky rain across the sea,
Dull pewter light, when suddenly
The level sun breaks through, makes clear
Another perfect hemisphere:
Its rainbow-self, supported by
A dark horizon, arcs the sky.
I watch the colours falter and,
Slipping on shingle, fall on sand.

Yet, high above the crumbling cliff,
A concrete pillbox stands as if
In crazy gesture of defence;
As if the huge indifference
Of change, decay, might somehow be
Perturbed by such small dignity
Which slowly shifts and cracks, and so
Will shatter on the stones below.

Search for a sound hypothesis:
'Safe as houses', 'Bank on this',
Dead clichés of security!
Houses? Bank? You'd better tie
Mementoes in a plastic bag,
Chuck in the sea, mark with a flag
The spot where fish or mermen may
With luck, remember you one day.

Our rented time is running out,
But unlike tide won't turn about
With regular and prompt dispatch
To land upon the beach fresh catch,
As gradually, with gathering pace,
Life ebbs out from the human race
Inhabiting a world grown ill.
Time for a benediction still:

Peace to the gulls and guillemots,
To curlews and their bleak mudflats,
To sea-birds, sea-anemones,
To marsh-plants, meadow butterflies,
To lavender and gorse and mallows,
To creatures of the depths and shallows;
Peace to the vast blue out-of-reach;
Peace to the stones on Thorpeness Beach.

Neil Powell

PAINTING WILTSHIRE BY SEASONS IN A REALISTIC RANGE OF SOFT COLOURS AND UNEXPECTED RHYMES

Sabled dabblers stretch spring canvases over
Heytesbury hills; Sap Green on Titanium White:
pointillist. Crocus easels the thaw, offers up the
thumb, slides across the sludge-grey-ochre weave,

wet on wet. Sherrington summer sun drips
Pollock gold on the glass of Wiltshire water.
Lapwings bristle-stroke Crockerton skies,
seep oily over the lime-framed edge of Shear.

Bidcombe stipples in autumn rust, bleeds
leaves from the slash of October's thrust;
oozes sepia sprigs through the crust of its
size, before winter glazes ground a matte

palette of sighs; peals through boughs, ravished
shrubbery shrill, tears pigment from Codford and the
Deverills; smudges on the fingerprint of another year,
then draws Ivory Black impasto over its own signature.

Chris Tutton

NUDE
after Willy Ronis, 'Nu provençal'

How simple it is: day knocks
And somebody opens, the shutter opens in
And in come light and warmth together as one and the same
And where she stands
Is neither a circle of privacy
Nor the arena of a performance
But only a small round mat for her feet on the cold tiles
While under an empty mirror
She bows to the water lifted in her hands
And sideways on her sunlight comes in from the garden
And on her back there is a man's admiration.

You will say it is only a picture, another nude
But I say it has been that simple:
Jug, basin, washstand, towel and chair
The plain nouns, and a woman at a meeting place
Of warm sunlight and loving admiration
And easy feeling both.

David Constantine

LENT

March, and the bailiff winds are at the door.
Alcohol, cigarettes all have to go. Abstain,
repent. No more meat or chocolate, no more
quietly obsessive checking of your phone
like the pulse of a slowly dying friend. Refrain.
No more taking photographs of pictures –
let the world go, like Michelangelo's sculpture
made of snow that no-one ever framed.

The house lies purged and empty. Still the winds blow.
Give up the wilderness, the wandering.
Retreat instead to that windless winter morning
when a young man stood in the gardens of the palazzo,
lips glistening, hair shining at the nape
before the bomb-blast of sun, not anyone's to keep.

Jane Draycott

CREATION
for Deb Mell

Who are these strange godbodies,
parrot-beaked and plural, lithe as fishes
swimming in sequinned waters? They shine
on the walls like icons,
grimace in pigment like cartoons.

For nearly a week
you've hardly broken off
to rest, or eat, your eyes ringed dark with shadow,
fingers drawing, painting, threading, cutting up
the plastic doll-heads, sticking on
the one-by-one of beads and sequins, keeping yourself awake
with pot after pot of coffee
and these are the result – this cold skin white
with the feather-prints of fingers, this plastic ear, this mouth,
this nostril, this open eye. They cry
as if with silent laughter, every orifice sealed shut
with varnish, choker at each throat
set hard. My finger's touch
can't hurt them. Water or blood or sweat
evaporates.

They draw back their closed stares;
their pouting lower lip
swells to a kind of kiss. This androgynous bird
swims on the paper; this winged fish
soars in a sky of glass.

Your lizard god is peering down on us
and seeing nothing,
flashing its fish- and-fowl
its male-and-female, its old and only
beginning.

Susan Wicks

LINE PLEASE

*A line is: a) a sick circle b) an unfolded word, c) an aggressive
dot d) what you want to erase e) what you regret after you dish
it out.* – Yoko Ono, 'Line Talk'

An aggressive dot stuttering now into morse,
now to Death's autograph on ECG monitors,

the point of this pen ploughing on from birth
to its boring verse-end half-rhyme of death.

What you regret. Inuit rage to Yoruba culture,
lines in land, flesh self-harmed into sculpture;

the trails left by my Oulipian rats in their maze
unravelling like a lie. *What you want to erase:*

those crumpled white sheets as if Cozens' ink
fell like a black sunlight on a page I'd wish blank,

its landscape folding under geological strain,
an unfolded word unfolding again and again,

my sick circle of mistakes on their Mōbius strip,
the repressed returning to read from its script,

my own spirit hesitating on a spiral stairway,
too late for all time with the right thing to say.

Ian Duhig

114

CUTTING IN

It's hard to know where to begin
all things being already in progress
the painting already alive before the first brush
is dipped before the first colour is mixed
from the marigolds lilacs poppies long after
they have lived long after the teenage gardener
sowed their seeds in the run-down remnants
of what his grandfather called the family home

–but whose story is this that insists
its weft into the canvas woven by the girl
in the tenth district while his seed rounded
her belly as she rounded into womanhood
and he in exploration of what it is to be he
steps back already proud of his work?

Anne Stewart

BABIES

There ought to be another word for babies.
Painters should paint them like women, the size
of continents, cloud formations, whales, Bacon
should have been their high priestess, specialised
in mounds of pink, primal soup of pink, muscled,
boned, straining away from buckles and braces,
dropped on all fours, teetering at odd angles
to exit from canvas, howling in cages.
There ought to be a God, capable of
metamorphosing into every hurdle
of a dream: a heel on the rung above
your hand, a Lucifer under your heel.
There ought to be a word, a God, for us:
us mothers, protectors, dreamers, creators.

Mimi Khalvati

THE SPIRAL PAINTER

Now I wait for you in altered oils,
framed, unframed, a little dark and
rubbed around the edges; dressed,

undressed, I caress you with the
edge of my finger.

Now I animate you in arcadian reflections;
colour still holds me,
neither of us is lost.

Now I retouch everything. The stammer, the
sough, the bits no-one else can see; beyond the
yellow varnish of the horizon, the impossible sky.

Chris Tutton

ROAST PEPPERS

Then the sunny kitchen
With its lemon tree, its generous

Pots and terracotta
Jardinières of basil,

Fills with a smoke of garlic
And roast red peppers.

Momentarily
Sinking between terraces,

The slant evening sun
Floods the little room.

Its fiery light illumines
Ochre walls, the antique

Crockery, the paintings,
Bowls of olives, lemons,

The sweet, sharp, blackened
Peppers, delicious.

Their biting sweetness
Melting on the tongue;

One last fierce gleam
Blazing from beyond

Ramshackle tenement,
Alley-way – haphazard,

Impermanent, our home,
The only one we have –

The ordinary world
With its austere demand:

Live. Be happy.

Katrina Porteous

HAND PAINTED

You'd be amazed at the height of the birch
you used to study from the bedroom.
Tall and spindly it outlives the wind.
I'm writing this with one of the pencils

you gave me at Taipei airport.
This is the last message it will write.

The other five worn down to thumb nail size.
Leaves are hand-painted on the wood,

cherry blossom in the spring.
The reason I started to write was watching

the birch from your window
where you'd lent on the sill in summer.

Last night in the sudden slant of storm
it seemed the tree would crash

into the greenhouse but it just bends further.
Nowhere to go.

HBs are cedar wood.
Hand painted leaves

will be locked in the drawer
to out-write all of us.

Wendy French

THE COOKHAM RESURRECTION

A boatload of the resurrected
trailing amazement,
cast off, second-chancing
from a Berkshire village.

See how hesitatingly
they renew acquaintance,
dipping earth-stained fingers
in the holy Thames.

Then home to homeliness,
a step up from the tow-path,
sure of their ground
and all they left behind.

To resume in the rinsed
clarity of vision what before
seemed daily, good bread
risen to angel food.

Going once more about
their business, love's
transfiguration of each trade
or sturdy labour

in a field of praise
contiguous with heaven
where the gate stands open
and they pass between.

John Mole

THE HILL ABOVE HARLECH
William Nicholson 1917

No person shall...make any photograph, sketch, plan, model
or other representation within any area...
Defence of the Realm Act, Jan 1916

The landscape was on the radio. It was early days
transmitting like that, but some things came through –
the fields, the shine of the slate rooves after the rain.

The artist added his voice: a map was the last thing
he'd wanted to make from the smoke near the cottages
crouched by the wood, the light the colour of tin.

But it was all just words. He'd wanted to show how the sky
was everything – the long roads, the pandemonium
and the lulls in the pandemonium, a complete guide.

Jane Draycott

WOMEN RUNNING

after Picasso: Deux femmes courant sur la plage

Look how their large bodies leaping
from dresses fill the beach, how their breasts
swing happiness, how the mediterraneans
of sea and sky fondle their flesh. Nothing

could rein them in. The blown wildnesses
of their dark animal hair, their hands joined
and raised, shout triumph. All their senses
are roused as they hurtle towards tomorrow.

That arm laid across the horizon,
the racing legs, an unstoppable quartet, pull
me from my skin and I become one of them,
believe I'm agile enough to run a mile,

believe I'm young again, believe age
has been stamped out. No wonder, I worship
at the altar of energy, not the energy huge
with hate which revels in tearing apart,

in crushing to dust but the momentum
which carries blood to the brain, these women
across the plage, lovers as they couple
and tugs at the future till it breaks into bloom.

Myra Schneider

LADDER

You text me a pen n' ink sketch
of a ladder that hovers over

> the world's number-crunching
> madness

and these ways we've found
to live our lives: coaches,
buses, cars, trains:

You're in transit from South
to North,
in commuting
back and forth across
the Pennines.

And your ladder is a
floating
smile –

> curved around us
> in my stone room.

And now and now?
We have these delicate,
hand-drawn rungs to each other.

Anne Caldwell

MOON, BIRD, MOUNTAIN

if the moon was full
we might miss
the glint in the bird's eye

and if the bird was white
we could lose
the aureole of blue light

and if it was day
we wouldn't notice
the mountain alive with heat

and we'd be less
for not standing
under a three-quarter moon

with a blackbird
on the edge of promise
fullness, flight

Lynne Rees

ACKNOWLEDGEMENTS

'About Face' by Patience Agbabi form "Metamorphosis: Poems inspired by Titian" (National Gallery 2002) 'I Would Like to be a Dot in a Painting by Miró' by Moniza Alvi from "Split World, Poems 1990-2005" (Bloodaxe Books 2008) 'Outsider Art' by Moniza Alvi from "Europa" (Bloodaxe Books 2008) 'Memories of Flight (Pictures at an Exhibition'by Roselle Angwin from "Looking for Icarus" (Bluechrome 2005) 'The Art of the Handkerchief' by Michael Bayley from "The Art of the Handkerchief" (Oversteps Books) 'Mean Squares' by Francesca Beard was originally commissioned by B3 Media for the Tate Online. 'Portrait of the Master with Missing Table'by Clare Best published in "The Interpreters House no 58, March 2015"'Painted Bird, Found in a Roman Grave' by Alison Brackenbury first published in "The Rialto" ''Monument' by Alison Brackenbury first published in "The North" 'Under the Vault' by Alison Brackenbury first published in "Snakeskin" 'Ice Age Art: an Exhibition' by Alison Brackenbury first published in "Stand" 'Nude' by David Constantine from "Something for the Ghosts" (Bloodaxe Books 2002) 'Dawn, Noon and Evening' by David Constantine from "Nine Fathoms Deep" (Bloodaxe Books 2009)

'Pruning the Magnolia' by John Daniel from "Skinning the Bull" (Oversteps Books) 'How Often Does it Happen' by Jane Draycott first published in International Gallerie (India) Issue 27, 2010 'The Imaginary Municipal Gallery Revisited' and 'Line Please' by Ian Duhig from "Digressions" (Smokestack Books)

'Two Nudes' and 'Cave Painting' by Linda France from "You are Her" (Arc 2010) 'Susan Martin, Painter's Wife' by Linda France from "Red" (Bloodaxe Books 1992) 'Self Portrait' and 'Polyphemus and Galata' by Linda France from "Storyville" (Bloodaxe Books 1997) 'Sunflowers' and 'Mauritsuis' by Wendy French from "Splintering the Dark" (Rockingham Press) 'Hand Painted' by Wendy French from "Surely you Know This" (Tall Lighthouse Press) 'An Inconsequential Photograph' first published in "Artemis".

'After Kandinsky; Yellow, Red, Blue (1925)' by Katherine Gallagher from "Carnival Edge: New and Selected Poems" (Arc Publications 2010

'Camomile Tea' by Gaia Holmes first published in theUniversity of Huddersfield Creative Writing Anthology 2006.

'Everywhere You See Her' by Mimi Khalvati from "Entries on Light" (Carcanet 1997) 'Babies by Mimi Khalvati from "The Chine" (Carcanet 2002)

'Woodland Burial' by Frances Leviston from "Metamorphosis; Poems Inspired by Titian" (National Gallery 2012)

'Cézanne to Monsieur Vollard' by John Mole first appeared in The European English Messenger 'The Gesture'by John Mole first appeared in The Spectator. 'The Cookham Resurrection' by John Mole from "For the Moment" Peterloo Poets. 2000.'Diana and Actaeon' by Sinéad Morrissey from"Metamorphosis;Poems Inspired by Titian" (National Gallery 2012)

'The Woodcarver' by Andrew Nightingale from "The Big Wheel" (Oversteps Books, www.overstepsbooks.com)

'Self Portrait with Cropped Hair' by Pascale Petite from "What the Water Gave Me" (Seren) 'Engine of History' by Katrina Porteous commissioned by the Poetry Society for Tate's OnlineMagazine, Tate Etc, May 2009. 'Sur La Terrace' and'The Stones on Thorpeness Beach' by Neil Powell from "Collected Poems" (Carcanet 1998)

A previous version of 'Fore Edge Painting' by Lynne Rees appeared in "Learning to Fall" (Parthian Books 2005)

'From the Lighthouse' by Lawrence Sail from "The Quick" (Bloodaxe Books 2015) 'Women Running' by Myra Schneider from "What Women Want" (Second Light Publications 2012)

'Titania Wings' by Susan Taylor from "The Suspension of Belief" (Oversteps Books) 'The Insoluable Harmonies of Colour' from "Angles Of Repose" (Avalanche Books 2012) A previous version of 'Painting Wiltshire by Seasons in a Realistic Range of Soft Colours and Unexpected Rhymes' by Chris Tutton from "Angles of Repose" (Avalanche Books 2012) and originally commissioned by The Warminster Villages Development Trust. 'Portrait in Fading Colours' by Chris Tutton from "Rain Angel" (Avalanche Books 2003)

'Ophelia Drowning in the Tate' by Simon Williams from "Quinks" (Oversteps Books 2006)